The
Professional's
Self-
Assessment
Kit

Michèle
Eckenschwiller

KOGAN PAGE

Kogan Page is the UK member of the Euro Business Publishing Network.
The European members are:
Les Editions d'Organisation, France; Verlag Moderne Industrie, Germany;
Liber, Sweden; Franco Angeli, Italy; and Deusto, Spain.
The Network has been established in response to the growing demand for
international business information and to make the work of Network authors
available in other European languages.

Les Editions d'Organisation, 1992
Translated by Ann Leonard
Illustrated by Sool Sbiera

First published in France in 1992 by
Les Editions d'Organisation, 26 avenue Emile-Zola, 75015 Paris,
entitled Vous et .... Vos Aspirations Professionnelles, ISBN 2-7081-1460-3

This edition first published in Great Britain in 1993 by
Kogan Page Ltd, 120 Pentonville Road, London Nl 9JN.

British Library Cataloguing in Publication Data.
A CIP record for this book is available from the British Library.

ISBN 0 7494 1047 7

DTP for Kogan Page by
Jeff Carter 197 South Croxted Road, London SE21 8AY

Printed in Great Britain by
Biddles Ltd, Guildford and Kings Lynn

TABLE OF CONTENTS

The following symbols are used throughout this book to indicate:

Find your way.

Fill it in.

INTRODUCTION

> *'To live is to change;*
> *To change is to mature;*
> *To mature is to be constantly recreated.'*
>
> Henri BERGSON

In this book we are going to put ourselves deliberately in a *practice* situation, where we can both put experience into practice and learn from it.[1]

Practice is a specific, repeated, deliberate activity, an intricate network of interactions between the individual – with his motivations, objectives and the means selected to achieve them – and his environment.[2] On one hand, practice has a collective quality, linked to an individual's social position. But it also has a unique, original quality: everybody acts in a particular way and feels that this is an expression of personal identity.

'Thus, from early childhood, through his family environment, an individual is provided with a set of characteristics which is in one sense structured by social context (cultural and family heritage) and in another sense structural, in that it generates and organizes practices and performances which can be objectively regulated.'[3]

Studying your own way of functioning helps you to be aware of the 'non-accidental' nature of this behaviour and understand that you are your own work tool.

So that you can analyze your professional behaviour, we offer, in the following pages, a series of themes, ideas and questions for you to work through.

Our aim is to help you choose the right questions to put to yourself, to select the right things for investigation.

This procedure goes hand in hand with a personal profile and if this means a step back into the past for you, remember that it also plays an important part in the present. We mean to supply you with everything that you need to understand your professional experience and to assess your mode of 'functioning'.[4]

This guide can support an individual assessment, and be equally useful as a basis for study in a training seminar on assessment. It provides, both for the assessor and the assessed, an opportunity for a new approach to appraisal.

Section 1
ANALYZE YOUR PROFESSIONAL BEHAVIOUR

'When you don't know what you're looking for,
You don't know what you'll find.'

L FEBVRE

We live in a time of increasingly rapid technological development, which entails much social change, so we all need to be equipped with a means of understanding and operating in this environment. In these changing circumstances, accepted behaviour is no longer always applicable to a professional situation. Therefore it is important that each of us considers, or reconsiders, his mode of 'functioning'.

Companies are being transformed under the influence of all kinds of technical innovation and various socio-economic changes. Markets fluctuate, in turn provoking rises or slumps in activity, and competition seems to be increasing.

New equipment calls for new prac-tices and new skills. Consider the development of computers, office automation, audio-visual aids, robots or the advances in the field of elec-tronics. Traditional professions are disappearing and new ones are tak-ing their place, altering qualification requirements.

As a result, companies have to devise strategies for better human resource management to facilitate the mobil-ity and redeployment of their staff.

In tandem with these upheavals in work methods, workers' attitudes have also changed to encompass a desire for expression and participa-tion. New attitudes to behaviour have appeared, affecting communi-cation methods as well as the func-tions of authority.

In such a situation, the individual needs to find meaning in his actions and to study his methods whether in the sphere of work, training or daily activities. He must try to pin down and clarify points of reference by which he can monitor his normal environment.

However, theoretical knowledge which is external and rigid is no longer satisfying. Established knowledge is not always enough to meet the demands of these changes; it is often superseded by experience in the field. It is generally accepted nowadays that there is a superior level of knowledge, and some people have it; far greater importance is given to experience and real-life situations.

On the one hand, it is now common practice to combine work experience programmes with degree course studies. On the other hand, a person's experience is taken into account in the framework of an education system based on the recognition of acquired skills.

It is a case of analyzing the difference between the theory of what you do and how you actually do it.

1

Describe the CONTEXT
of your professional behaviour

FOR TODAY'S SOCIETY	FOR YOUR COMPANY	FOR YOU
– Changing economic and technical environment		
– Rapid social change		
– Increasing competition		
– Unstable employment situation		
– Need for new knowledge ('learning') and/ or skills ('know-how' and 'social skills')		
– Change in structure of qualification requirements		
– New inter-personal behaviour		

We live in a world of doubt and contradiction so we need to find a new rationale for living. We need to take a step back and examine how we live, investigate alternative routes to the establishment of innovative structures for the creation of new social relations, new decision-making methods. Each of us must discover his own individual pattern, develop his own style.

It is becoming more crucial to value knowledge gained through experience on a technical as well as a social level. It involves equipping oneself with the means to substantiate knowledge gained in the field, to analyze and transmit it.

This work experience, combined with established knowledge, enhances and completes one's knowledge while calling it into question.

The human element is accentuated in today's companies. Alongside the practical management of the work to be done, the human resources that do the work need to be managed.

The problems of job rotation, change and career development can only be controlled by a continuous review of collective and individual skills. It is in this context that a framework of deliberate observation of work practices is proposed.

This can be included in an assessment study or can be conducted separately. It gives an insight into an individual's role at a particular point, and can be the basis for a 'check-up' or appraisal.

By discovering peoples' personal skills, you enable them to perform better and more efficiently, and allow them to fulfil their potential.

By recognizing the quality of his experience and appraising his performance, the individual discovers his true identity and his place in society. He can thus improve his skills on a theoretical and a practical level, and live a fuller life.

In a climate of confidence and mutual trust, this work can enhance the individual's development and be included in the policy for change in a company's organizational structure.

It is in line with the basic objectives of an annual review:

- to begin a dialogue and solve problems highlighted in the evaluation study, and identify behaviour which could block projects in the future;

- to serve as the basis for the forward-looking management of personnel by paying attention to any expressed requirements and employees' development potential. [5]

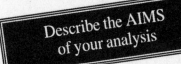

Describe the AIMS of your analysis

FOR COMPANIES *in general*	FOR YOUR COMPANY *in particular*	FOR THE INDIVIDUAL *in general*	FOR YOU
– To adapt to the environment		– To control one's job and the course of one's professional career	
– To establish a forward-looking management attitude to employment		– To increase the possibilities for professional mobility and the opportunities for promotion in one's present company or in another	

This review is thus the ideal opportunity to discuss technical points and also to investigate the social aspects of work, with its value systems, norms and aims.

In a general way, taking methods of work as a subject of study helps each of us to:
- address the basis of our own identity;
- clarify our relationship to the environment;
- structure or restructure our behaviour and way of thinking;
- have our experience recognized;
- think about possible improvements.

This process involves distancing and integrating ourselves, an attempt to undergo deconditioning and the construction of new systems which we will develop over the following pages.

These ideas will probably appeal to individuals on a personal level but they are also addressed to all those professionals concerned with the development of human potential: training instructors, consultants, those responsible for human resources, company executives, etc.

3

Describe the OBJECTIVES of your analysis

FOR COMPANIES *in general*	FOR YOUR COMPANY *in particular*	FOR THE INDIVIDUAL *in general*	FOR YOU
– To maximize every-body's potential		– To discover one's professional identity	
– To award relevant qualifications		– To be able to under-stand oneself and take action	
– To facilitate the mobility and rede-ployment of staff		– To enhance one's experience	
– To develop dialogue within the company		– To become aware of one's personal and professional poten-tial	
– To motivate staff		– To become more autonomous and responsible	

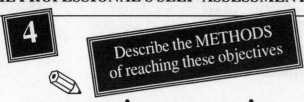

4

Describe the METHODS
of reaching these objectives

FOR COMPANIES *in general*	FOR YOUR COMPANY *in particular*	FOR THE INDIVIDUAL *in general*	FOR YOU
– To analyze change and establish a system for professional activities with an outward-looking perspective		– To clarify one's relationship with the environment	
		– To analyze one's behaviour	
– To evaluate individual and collective ability		– To discover one's professional situation	
– To value knowledge gained through experience		– To devise a personal professional project	
– To develop and manage professional potential		– Self-development	
– To set up training projects			

Section 2
DISCOVER THE ORIGIN AND SIGNIFICANCE OF YOUR PROFESSIONAL BEHAVIOUR

'A river, like the story of life, is made up of currents.

'These currents are seen and experienced in a given time and place. But they draw their force, their energy from the uphill and downhill slopes, and from the banks, the edges which frame them, channel them by imposing precise movements.

'The uphill slope is the source, the birth, the past ever present and active, with its tributaries, its inspirations, its rainfall, the territories crossed, its dams, seasons and sunshine.

'The downhill slope is the distance which separates us from the end of the river, the future with all its developments, projects, rejections, openings, losses, death, transformation and renewal.

'The banks are our limits, our demarcation lines, which hold back the currents, but which lend them their shape, their force, their colour, their landscape.'

Gaston PINEAU

Analyzing our professional behaviour gives us an inner, personal wisdom about reality, and enables us to interpret our behaviour in a given situation.

The world in which we live tends to supply us with a set of preconceived notions as well as modes of conduct which we try, with greater or lesser degrees of success, to adjust to our own experience, distorting that experience in the process if necessary. We often end up with inadequate images, sketchy or irrelevant outlines of ideas.

Therefore, we must be consistent about word and fact, about what is said and the material world around us, by resisting the pressure to conform, by looking afresh at real life. We all develop a method shaped by our past, by the way in which we have progressively shaped our personality.

Certain psychologists use the image of the tree to represent personal development.[6] This symbol is used here but with a new twist: our tree takes 'root' in a certain place; it feeds on man's universal characteristics. To a certain extent these are decided by innate factors, hereditary characteristics, sex, physiological and morphological aspects.

A small shoot appears – it has not chosen the time or place or its characteristics. The 'trunk' will gradually thicken, grow bigger and strengthen its position, nurtured by its environment: family, school, leisure companions... Fertilizers are applied (knowledge, books, the media...) but so are poisons (bad influences). It can fall victim to parasites, be hurt or contract diseases causing more or less significant scarring.

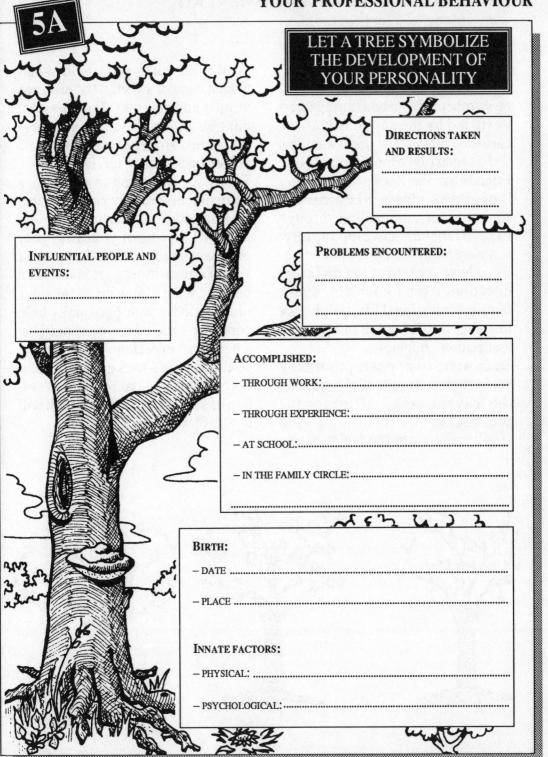

5A

LET A TREE SYMBOLIZE THE DEVELOPMENT OF YOUR PERSONALITY

DIRECTIONS TAKEN AND RESULTS:

....

....

INFLUENTIAL PEOPLE AND EVENTS:

....

....

PROBLEMS ENCOUNTERED:

....

....

ACCOMPLISHED:

– THROUGH WORK: ....

– THROUGH EXPERIENCE: ....

– AT SCHOOL: ....

– IN THE FAMILY CIRCLE: ....

....

BIRTH:

– DATE ....

– PLACE ....

INNATE FACTORS:

– PHYSICAL: ....

– PSYCHOLOGICAL: ....

Now a shrub needs support (standards, rules of conduct) but must not be smothered by neighbouring trees. Fortified by the sap (motivation, curiosity, interests) it needs sun, rain and oxygen (the people around you). Friends like the woodpecker relieve it of grubs – others, like birds and squirrels, are companions through life. 'Branches' develop rapidly; some are hardy, others are more fragile. These represent the different directions taken by our tree: study, family, professional life, political or union activities, club or sporting associations, hobbies…

Buds start to appear, promising achievement or potential, and then the leaves emerge, affirming the presence of life in our tree. And finally, there are the fruits, some good, some not so good, wild or cultivated, sour or sweet… but each one unique and original. Time passes: our tree knows fine days, weathers the storms. Branches break off or are pruned back; others survive.

Today we are going to examine a particular branch of *your* tree – that of your professional behaviour.

As in all aspects of your life, your professional situation is the result of social conditioning. It is decided both by what you want to be, your ideal, built on your personally held concepts – and what you should be, what others expect of you. Based on your life story – background, education, experience – you build up a system of values for yourself which will in turn dictate your behaviour.

PERSONAL NOTES

YOUR TREE

Having considered this section on 'your tree', what comments or remarks would you like to make about your development?

You respect certain attitudes and you condemn others. Depending on circumstances, you will adopt one or several roles, determined by your status and the self-image that you wish to project.

We all more or less drift along in our character stereotypes: 'Character is not the individual who we are, but who we would like to convince others that we are, or then again, who others would like to convince us that we are.'[7]

We notice that certain attitudes are associated solely with convention – the done thing – or appearances, which are the 'shrouds of convention'.[8] We disappear behind masks of conformity, opportunism or cynicism.

We may cling to modes of conduct as shields to allow us to escape the anguish of being just ourselves. In this way, the 'mock serious' or the 'limited specialist' hides a variety of deficiencies or failures.

Thus, taking our professional functioning as a subject of study should afford us an opportunity to think about the fundamentals of our behaviour, to understand better certain attitudes and to evaluate the why and how of our actions.

Section 3
PUT YOUR PROFESSIONAL LIFE UNDER THE MICROSCOPE: OBSERVE AND NOTE

> *'We should observe in many ways, all the while delaying judgement.'*
> Jean-Guy NADEAU

Professional experience can provide an opportunity for research for the individual. Working on yourself, and in particular on an analysis of your job, involves being ready to do some research.

First, it is a case of being interested in the object of your study, being committed and feeling involved. For this you must be ready to 'live with' your research by making time for it in your daily life. It is not, however, a case of letting yourself be swamped or overwhelmed by too many questions. Your activity must be contained, directed, disciplined. To analyze your professional behaviour you must acquire method, tools and set targets. The *observation phase* distances us from our experience, while giving us a sense of wariness about our profession.

1 GENERAL OBSERVATION

First, make a note of what must be done to collect all the raw material, the information about the various tasks you perform. This approach needs a certain frame of mind, a shifting of mental parameters. You become the subject of your own observation, while developing your self-assessment abilities.

21

You become both the object of observation and the researcher by showing an interest in what you do right now.

Make a summary of your work and this could start the whole process. Begin to compile a list of what you do all day, jotting down any observations or remarks about your job as they spring to mind.

If you like, you could use the blank pages at the end of this book – they are intended for this very purpose. The idea of this diary of events is to avoid missing information and give you more freedom. Noting these things in writing is, to an extent, to 'own' them, which is reassuring and leaves you free for other observations. On the other hand, the need to find the correct word or phrase for a clear explanation requires disciplined effort.

If you find it easier, you could record your thoughts, or photograph yourself or film yourself... in other words, use anything to gather the information... but above all, reserve judgement; don't automatically censure your findings.

PERSONAL NOTES

GIVE A SUMMARY OF YOUR PROFESSIONAL LIFE

Try to put your professional life into words:
– analyze what is involved in your work;
– list your key activities;
– note any problems you have, whether they involve the work itself or are
  more general;
– note your ambitions, what you are pleased about (hopes, expectations, projects).

2 METHODICAL AND SYSTEMATIC OBSERVATION

You will quickly realize that you need tools for your analysis and that you have to be methodical. Graphs and questionnaires can help you here.

Fill in the graph opposite over a fixed period of time, so that it reflects accurately your working life – a period of at least a week or two is appropriate.

Record all the jobs you do, specifying when you did them (time and date), what they were, where you did them, how long they took, what you used to do them, any work partners, and why you did them. In the 'remarks' column, note your appraisal, opinions and suggestions. Reading over this record will allow you to allot a particular time to your activities (duration and hourly breakdown), the place (area of operation), and also to specify what you want to do. You will end up with a kind of photo-kit of your activity, and it will be up to you to expand each point:

– what?
– where?
– when?
– how?
– with whom?
– why?

You will arrive at your own conclusions when you respond to a number of key questions.

ANALYZE YOUR PROFESSIONAL LIFE

DATE/ TIME	TASK	PLACE(S)	AIDS EQUIPMENT METHOD(S)	PARTNER(S)	PURPOSE/ REMARKS/ TIME TAKEN

Section 4
DRAW UP YOUR SIX-POINT PROFESSIONAL DIAGNOSIS

> '*Look with all your eyes, look.*'
>
> Jules VERNE

You have been making observations and notes on your professional behaviour on a daily basis, building up a file of information. You are now in a position to take a step back from this. You are in possession of information which allows you to draw certain conclusions and engage in a problem-solving exercise; in other words, you must distance yourself from events and take an overview.

'WHAT?': YOUR SKILLS

What you have put under the heading 'Task' in chart 7 allows you to break down your activity in response to a twofold question:
– What do I do? About what? This analysis should be thorough and will involve you in specifying the content of each of your various tasks and their degree of importance in terms of time taken. You will thus be able to identify on a daily, weekly, monthly or annual basis the various abilities associated with your job and the assignments and responsibilities you have undertaken. Then you will be able to regroup your activities under the following headings:

Examples:
- Preparation
- Execution
- Coordination
- Management
- Information
- Inter-personal relations
  (telephone conversations)
- Meetings
- Training
- Control, help, follow-up
- Reporting
- Decision-making

You can then study the breakdown. This can be done over a week, a fortnight or even a month, and notes can be made under the heading 'Time taken' in chart 7. Thus you can make the transition from a superficial description of your work to an analytical account. The key tasks associated with your job have been identified and can now be studied in detail.

You can ask yourself:

- Which task is the most important in terms of priority?
- Which is the most unnecessary?
- What aspects of your job reflect your abilities?

- What causes you problems, or shouldn't involve you at all?
- Which tasks seem irrelevant or obsolete?
- What new methods should be put into operation?

In this way you can discover whether you allocate too much time to one area of your work while neglecting or ignoring another.

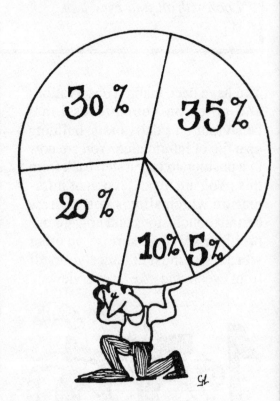

WHAT ARE YOUR TASKS?

Look at chart 7 again and draw up a list of your tasks, noting how often they occur. Some may not appear on the chart if they only happen monthly, annually or in exceptional circumstances but refer to them anyway.

TASKS

DAILY	WEEKLY	MONTHLY	ANNUAL	EXCEPTIONAL

Sort out the main parameters of your work by grouping your activities under headings:

– ....

– ....

– ....

– ....

– ....

– ....

'WHERE?': YOUR SPACE

The column 'Place(s)' will help you to picture your experience in terms of your own space and how you use it. From this, you will see that you tend to give priority to certain types of incoming information over others.[9]

Do you remember the scene from Peter Weir's film *Dead Poets Society* where the teacher asks each pupil in turn to stand on his desk? This gives them a completely different perspective of the classroom.

Thus, depending on the place you occupy, you are sensitive to a selection system based on a collection of sensory stimuli (sight, hearing, sense of smell and touch). You will see, hear, smell and touch things from a fixed vantage point.

You will also develop a new strategy with regard to relationships. You will find that you are closer to some people; that it is easier to communicate with some of your colleagues. Your relationships with your peers will evolve around the way you use that space. You will be on intimate terms with John who shares your office, but you only meet Bill who occupies a corner at the end of the corridor occasionally. In this way a sort of selective reinforcement of your communication system operates, bringing with it varying degrees of emotional involvement.

Moreover, if the choice of a location is dictated by your business, your business in turn is influenced by location.

We can even draw a further distinction between your *kinaesthetic* and your *tactile* space.[10] The space we have at our disposal either inhibits or encourages certain activities. We may be restricted by too cramped a space, or feel that we cannot turn round or that there isn't enough room to swing a cat (kinaesthetic space).

BREAKDOWN OF ACTIVITES BY CATEGORY DURING:

– week [　　　　] – fortnight [　　　　] – month [　　　　]

Percentage

Category of
activity

5%

– Your notes: ....

....

....

Add to this the necessity to respect the 'personal space' between one person and another; we do not like having to live at too close quarters – this is seen as a violation of our privacy (tactile space). Consequently, the working conditions of our jobs have a direct bearing on our behaviour. So we have to think, and think hard, about the places where we work – how we use this space – but also about how it is laid out (furniture, decor, colours, etc).

This in turn will lead to a consideration of the physical or physiological conditions of your job:

– what your space is like and the effect it has on you in a positive or negative sense (calm or commotion, stationary or moving about, balanced or overworked, human contact or isolation);

– physical factors such as noise, lighting, vibration, heat or cold, humidity or dust, etc, and their impact;

– the gestures and postures that your profession entails and the specific problems that they can cause (nervous fatigue, digestive problems, breathing problems, circulatory problems, auditory or visual difficulties, skin problems, backache, etc);

– the possible risks associated with machinery in the workplace (the dangers in a building site or workshop, for example).

Thinking about the way in which you occupy and manage your space will lead you to analyze your work areas in terms of ergonomics. In order to do this, you will have to fine-tune your faculties of observation and apply this maxim of Jules Verne:

'Look with all your eyes, look.'

YOUR SPACE IN 12 QUESTIONS

☞ Which of your workplaces are:
– usual?
– occasional?
– favourite?

☞ Does the geographical setting of these places seem:
Very satisfactory? ❑   Satisfactory? ❑   Unsatisfactory? ❑

☞ Within the workplace does the position of your space seem:
Very satisfactory? ❑   Satisfactory? ❑   Unsatisfactory? ❑

☞ Do you have at your disposal a space which is:
Inadequate? ❑   Adequate? ❑   Absolutely fine? ❑

☞ Does the quality of this space (lighting, sound-proofing, temperature and ventilation) seem:
Very satisfactory? ❑   Satisfactory? ❑   Unsatisfactory? ❑

☞ Are the furniture and decor:
Very pleasant? ❑   Appropriate? ❑   Unsatisfactory? ❑

☞ Is your storage space, in your opinion:
Very practical? ❑   Satisfactory? ❑   Unsatisfactory? ❑

☞ Do you have difficulties with the physical organization of your workplace(s)? If so, what are they?..

☞ What does this physical organization entail? ....

☞ What restraints does this same organization impose? ....

☞ Does your physical environment affect how you do your job? If so, how? ....

☞ Do improvements to your work space seem:
Uncalled for? ❑   Conceivable? ❑   Necessary? ❑

'WHEN?': YOUR TIME

To have the time – To not have the time – To take the time – To be short of time – To need more time – To run out of time…

Our whole life, be it in a professional or a private sense, organizes itself around time, the main axis of all our activities.

Time isn't elastic; it is the same for all of us – yet certain people seem to have more of it than others, or perhaps use it better. An argument or a pretext, an alibi or a defence, the lack of time or the pressure of time are constant complaints.

So, how do *you* manage this precious commodity?

We all live according to personal rhythms. We are all programmed by an internal biological clock, and so we are more effective at work on certain days of the week or at certain times of the day. You are, for instance, either a 'morning person' or an 'evening person'.

Moreover, the theory of biorhythms teaches us that, throughout our lives, three cycles (a physical cycle, an emotional cycle and a cerebral cycle)

influence our behaviour. We regularly go through positive or negative periods, but we also have important days where risks, physical, emotional or cerebral, are more significant.[11]

Even if we relate the meaning of this to the influence of our personality or our environment, we all freely refer to the 'highs' and the 'lows' in our behaviour, days when we 'have it' and days when we don't. It would be interesting to think about this, and pinpoint the time that is most favourable to the undertaking of an important task.

No doubt your social life imposes time constraints on you, but even here it is possible for you to manage this time instead of being a slave to it.

Read the notes you made in the columns 'Date/time' and 'Time taken' on chart 7 on page 25 and study the breakdown of your tasks.

This might be a revelation to you as it highlights the actual amount of time taken up by your various activities as well as the times at which you carry them out.

You will perhaps pinpoint some distractions: saturation points, time-wasting, interruptions, bad habits, etc.

YOUR TIME IN 12 QUESTIONS

In your professional life:

☞ Are you satisfied with the breakdown of your jobs and the time devoted to each?

Yes ☐   No ☐

☞ Have you identified distractions in your timetable?

Yes ☐   No ☐

If so, which?..

☞ Are you more efficient:

– at certain times of the day?   Yes ☐   No ☐

– certain days?   Yes ☐   No ☐

☞ Do you plan:

– your day?   Yes ☐   No ☐

– your week?   Yes ☐   No ☐

☞ Do you keep a diary?   Yes ☐   No ☐

If so, do you stick to it?   Yes ☐   No ☐

☞ Do you make a list of priorities with urgent business at the top?   Yes ☐   No ☐

☞ Do you manage to deal with the unexpected?   Yes ☐   No ☐

☞ Do you delegate?

Satisfactorily? ☐   Too much? ☐   Not enough? ☐

☞ Do you know how to say 'no' to non-priority demands?   Yes ☐   No ☐

☞ Do you have time for 'quiet time' (to think or read)?   Yes ☐   No ☐

☞ Do you manage to safeguard your private life?   Yes ☐   No ☐

☞ Do you feel under pressure because of lack of time?   Yes ☐   No ☐

This analysis will prompt you to ask yourself some questions about the way in which you live and how you arrange your time. After this exercise it is up to you to identify any changes to be made to your timetable. It is up to you to establish a set of priorities based on your objectives. In order to do this why not make a list of things to do and a corresponding time-plan? Re-read your list regularly, noting what has been done and making adjustments: reports, cancellations, etc.

– Learn to avoid being swamped by unnecessary work.
– Avoid rushing things. Some matters should be left to mature.
– Get chores out of the way by doing them as quickly as possible.

You will gradually learn to be more in control of your time.

Many seminars and publications deal with the topic of time management and they can provide valuable help.[12, 13]

You can think about adapting your timetabling as well as your daily, weekly, monthly or yearly routines:

– Do you allow a little flexibility in the organization of your time?
– Have you got the balance right between work and time for rest and relaxation?
– Do you think you use time well?

'Days may seem the same to a clock, but not to a man.'

Marcel PROUST

WHAT ARE YOUR WORK PROCEDURES?

AIDS EQUIPMENT METHOD(S)	DEGREE OF USE *(from 1, very little, to 5, very often)*					REMARKS
	1	2	3	4	5	

'HOW?': YOUR AIDS, EQUIPMENT AND METHODS

Here you are working with the information given under the heading in chart 7 (page25) about analyzing your professional life. You are going to look at the way in which you operate, how you usually do your work.

For this we suggest that you draw up a list of your usual methods, and then note their usefulness. Certain work modes will seem very important, while other procedures will only be used rarely or in exceptional circumstances.

In this way you can sort out:
- the equipment used;
- the methods imposed by your work station (instructions, prescribed operational procedures, etc);
- control systems (by whom, when, where and how your work is controlled);
- the amount of initiative you can show.

This analysis, together with your own observations, will enable you to be critical of your methods. Then you can concentrate on the difficulties or the deficiencies of your equipment or organizational methods. You can also challenge any outdated or extraneous procedures. You will be able to pinpoint any oddities in your routine and any personal or collective disharmony.

Where logic and efficiency are concerned, you will have to consider them as objectively as possible, drawing on your open-mindedness and your common sense.

Moreover, this exercise will enable you to isolate, from the detailed information gathered, what is required in order to hold down your job, mobilized knowledge, that is, knowledge which is actively applied in a situation, in terms of:

- *learning*: theoretical knowledge (mathematical, scientific, literary or technical), knowledge of a discipline (eg economics, law, computer science), knowledge of products, methods, languages (eg knowledge of a new accounting plan, of software programs, of the basics of industrial design);
- *know-how*: practical experience, a particular aptitude (eg the ability to speak French, how to work a machine, how to apply a method);
- *social skills*: linked with personal attitude, behaviour, the ability to adapt, sociability (eg the ability to lead a team, commercial sensitivity, responsibilities).

WHAT DOES YOUR JOB DEMAND?

MOBILIZED KNOWLEDGE	STRONG POINTS AND WEAK POINTS (from 1, very weak, to 5, excellent)					REMARKS
	1	2	3	4	5	
– Learning, knowledge:						
– Know-how:						
– Social skills:						

Now you have to think about these demands and evaluate your level for each type of requisite knowledge by drawing up your strong and weak points.

'WITH WHOM?': YOUR PARTNERS

Studying the entries for the column 'Partner(s)' in chart 7 (page 25) will help you to analyze your work from an inter-personal point of view. You are going to list the main partners in your professional circle, colleagues or others, who occupy upper or lower rungs of the hierarchical ladder. You can push this investigation a little further by undertaking a quantitative investigation of your communication with these people over a given period (see chart 14 opposite). In this way you will be able to illustrate your inter-personal network by representing the scale and importance of your involvement with your colleagues in a series of circles intersecting with your own. This will show just who you communicate with most, on average or merely occasionally, and those whom you meet rarely or whom you avoid. From this illustration we can make a qualitative assessment. You should consider:

– on the one hand, the positive reactions you provoke – confidence, sympathy, cooperation – or the negative reactions – defensiveness, fear or rejection, and the feelings you evoke;

WHAT IS YOUR RELATIONSHIP NETWORK?

Having sorted out who your main working partners are (see chart 7, page 25), tick each meeting with them over a given period (eg a week):

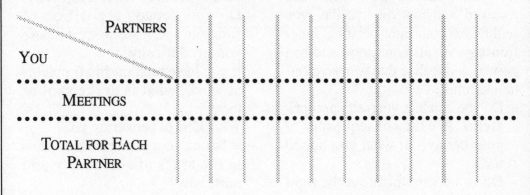

Put each partner in the circle corresponding to the frequency of your meetings.

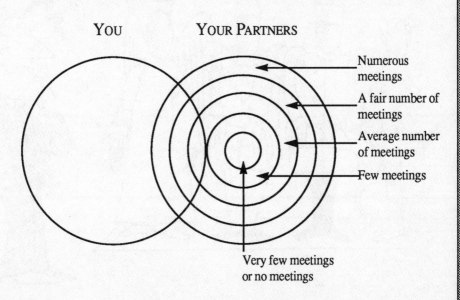

– on the other hand, the way in which you perceive things, your degree of openness and tolerance, but also your positive and negative attitudes.

As you analyze how you 'are received' and how you 'receive', you will reveal your inter-personal functioning with all your good and bad points, and realize that you have certain failings:

– Do you conduct yourself appropriately? Are the consequences of your behaviour what you hoped for?

– Do you communicate at the right level?

– Do you get on well with your colleagues?

– Do you feel that you are appreciated?

– What style of management does your boss have? Does it suit you?

– Do you occupy a position of authority and, if so, does this cause you any difficulty?

– If you have relationship problems at work, what is at the root of them?

– What kind of person are you?

– What are your main characteristics in the areas of sociability and sensitivity?

HOW DO YOU RELATE TO OTHERS?

In the area of relationships, the traits which characterize your behaviour are the following:
(For each trait, place a tick in the column of your choice.)

	WITH EASE	WITH DIFFICULTY
– you express yourself orally:		
• in an individual exchange		
• in a small group		
• in public		
• with your superiors		
– you write memos and reports		
– when working in a team, you cooperate		
– you lead and make others follow		
– you give orders		
– you take responsibility or you take the initiative		
– you are available; you listen		
– you withstand conflict or stress		
– you become annoyed and aggressive		
– you have faith in others and delegate		
– you inspire positive feelings		
– you provoke situations of distrust or tension		
– you help and encourage		
– you relax the atmosphere; you lark about		
– you judge others		
– you ask for help		

You are now in a position to look at things from another angle, to put yourself in a team by outlining the roles you play and also the roles that others would like you to play, or that convention obliges you to play. Chart 15 will help you to study your inter-personal behaviour. It will help you to understand better the quality of communication in your activities. Here you are touching on the psycho-social conditions of your work by highlighting the type of relationships that you have with your peers, superiors and subordinates. This will help you to have a keener understanding of the emotions engendered by you and your colleagues, and perhaps rationalize them, be they positive emotions (joy, pleasure, curiosity, encouragement) or negative ones (fear, anger, sadness, discouragement).

'WHY?': YOUR PURPOSE

In order to finish this exercise we must analyze the purpose of your job. It is, in fact, purpose which lends meaning to action, so long as it is accompanied by one or more short- or long-term objectives.

This study should be carried out on two levels:
- for your company;
- for yourself.

Therefore, you have to find out:
- your job objectives, and what the company expects of your job function;
- what your own expectations are *vis-à-vis* your job.

After drawing up a list of your personal qualities (what?), the procedures necessary (how?), the purposes (why?), it is possible to deduce your company's strategy with regard to your job function.

A definition of job function involves a definition of mission before clearly establishing:
- responsibilities;
- objectives;
- restrictions (time limits, means available, etc).

By using the data from chart 7 as well as the study of your qualities, you can, for each category of tasks needed for your job, outline your degree of responsibility, the objective(s), the constraints, but also the outcome of the work done and the consequences of any errors in the product or service.

By determining the scope of your participation within the company, you confirm your position as a link in the chain of a professional group.

You measure the extent of your involvement and highlight your role(s) from the work viewpoint (the relationship between your knowledge and experience) and that of behaviour (personal and interpersonal).

You are defining your responsibilities with regard to:
- machinery and equipment;
- products;
- security;
- professional partners.

You are building up a profile of your job with all the demands and resources it calls for. Therefore it is by analyzing your expectations (linked to your personal objectives) that you are going to see the correlation between your ambitions and those of the company, and measure any disparity.

WHAT IS YOUR FUNCTION?

TASKS CARRIED OUT (by category)	RESPONSIBILITIES AND INITIATIVES TO BE TAKEN			
	BY YOU	BY YOUR SUPERIORS	BY YOUR TEAM	BY OTHERS

What your company expects in particular from your work and from you:

...WHAT IS YOUR FUNCTION?

OBJECTIVES	RESTRICTIONS	OUTCOME OF YOUR WORK	CONSEQUENCES OF ERRORS	
			FOR YOU	FOR THE COMPANY

This touches on three areas still to be explored:

- your expectations related to the nature of the tasks to be carried out and how they tie in with the interests you want to develop (technical, scientific, artistic, etc);
- your material expectations – working conditions (rank, hours, leave, etc), and concrete considerations (salary, wages, benefits, etc);
- your social and psychological expectations based on your desired status.

Distancing yourself from the daily run of things is a way of putting your professional life into perspective, and reveals feelings of satisfaction or dissatisfaction. You understand better exactly why you feel that things are running smoothly, or otherwise, at work or why you have certain reservations. At the end of this chapter, the systematic breakdown of your professional life represents an analysis of your problems. The different elements are organized and categorized. To go any further you must understand the way you work by interpreting the results of your analysis and by establishing a system of relevant factors.

WHAT ARE YOUR PERSONAL EXPECTATIONS?

	VERY MODEST	MODEST	AVERAGE	GREAT	UNLIMITED
EXPECTATIONS LINKED TO INTERESTS:					
Technical					
Scientific					
Literary					
Artistic					
Administrative					
Numerical					
Social					
Sporting					
Educational					
Commercial					
Other:...................................					
....					
MATERIAL EXPECTATIONS					
Rank or position					
Hours, holidays					
Salary					
Promotional prospects					
Training prospects					
Mobility					
Social welfare					
Material benefits					
Other:..................................					
....					
EXPECTATIONS OF A SOCIAL OR PSYCHOLOGICAL NATURE					
Security					
Integration, belonging					
Responsibility					
Recognition					
Self-fulfilment					
Autonomy, independence					
Power					
Initiative, creativity					
Prestige					
Altruism, dedication					
Other:..................................					
....					

Section 5
UNDERSTAND YOUR PROFESSIONAL SITUATION

> '...for want of solving the problem, he was able to understand the situation, which wasn't so bad.'
>
> Philippe DJIAN

Following on from this phase of problem-solving, you must try to understand the way in which you live your professional life, how you are implicated in a whole network of inter-personal relations. First, it is not only a question of examining your way of working and the reference systems you call on when working, but also beliefs and preconceived notions. This leads you straightaway to a two-fold question:

– what are your models, your reference points, not only in the area of actual knowledge but also know-how and awareness of appropriate behaviour?

– what are the values that you respect?

MODELS AND VALUES

To study the ideals behind your professional practice, we must analyze your concepts, in order to know exactly on what your ideas of your profession are founded. Social concepts are the way in which man 'constructs his reality'.[14]

Each of us organizes our mental universe into coherent patterns, based on the knowledge gained through experience.

'For each group, social concepts are an appropriation of the outside world, a search for a direction, a starting point.'[15]

Intellectual factors blend with emotional factors and connect with the relationships we form with others within a social group.

Your perception of the world is selective; it is directed by needs, motivations and individual expectations. It also varies according to social background, each group having its own set of norms which influence the individual, dictate attitudes, and supply beliefs, opinions and stereotypes. It is consequently worthwhile investigating the foundations of our concepts to uncover their individual and social significance (see chart 18).

From this you will be in a position to identify your ultimate value system as it relates to your work and the bearing it has on your professional behaviour. A person's values can be classified in three categories relating to:
– identity;
– relationships;
– power.[16]

By taking a look at yourself from the point of view of your personal expectations combined with these three main value categories, you will highlight what is important for you and what prompts your behaviour; you will discover the key to your actions. Is it:
– identity: in other words what distinguishes you as a unique being with your own personal characteristics?
– relationships: in other words, your dealings with others, the type of attachments you make, your emotional and moral influence?
– power: in other words, everything that empowers you and allows you some kind of superiority?

HOW DID YOU COME TO CHOOSE YOUR PROFESSION?

☞ Did *you* choose your profession?

Yes ❑   No ❑   More or less ❑

☞ If so, why?..

☞ Does it correspond to your studies?

Completely ❑   To a certain extent ❑   Not at all ❑

☞ Were one or more members of your social circle already involved with it or a similar profession?

Yes ❑   No ❑

☞ What preconceived ideas of your profession did you have in terms of:

– learning?..

– know-how?..

– social skills?...

☞ Have these images developed?

Yes ❑   No ❑

☞ If so, how?

☞ In your professional life, have you been, or are you, influenced by one or more role models?

Yes ❑   No ❑

☞ If so, what were their principal traits and in what way have they influenced your professional style?..

....

HABITS AND CONMDITIONING

We may be creatures of habit, but that does not mean that we are aware of our routines. We talk about being conditioned by our job, meaning our repetitive habits. We tend to look for situations where the procedures are comfortingly familiar, while avoiding those which offer uncertainties.

A ritual is established:

- on the one hand, the social group we mix with have collective customs (eg style of greeting, tolerance *vis-à-vis* working hours, ways of relating dictated by profession and socio-cultural background);
- on the other hand, in keeping with these customs, we are apt to adopt individual habits, as much in our work methods as in our way of relating to those around us.

This ritual, which offers a kind of security, a framework, by dictating behaviour, involves a certain code of behaviour. In every group you will come across instances of the 'stated' and the 'unstated', and a respect for formal, and also informal, regulations which allow everyone to satisfy their key needs: to be recognized,

integrated and accepted. Moreover, through this repetition, we expand our experiential knowledge. However, in the long term this could turn out to be ponderous and inappropriate if not regularly challenged. We no longer think about these actions – they become automatic, and sometimes have to be endured rather than carried out voluntarily. We tend to remain cloistered, or allow ourselves to be typecast, within these roles, to 'play along' with the job with a series of 'formulas' and 'sure-fire recipes'. We are acting in accordance with what we are, what we want to do and what we think we ought to do, but our behaviour runs the risk of becoming out of date, even unacceptable. Professions evolve all the time and demand constant adaptation. This is why we suggest that you look at chart 20,[17] to understand your behaviour at work and the reactions you provoke in your professional circle. In this context, read your business diary or timetable and see how it affects your professional conditioning. We suggest that you list your main habits and try to define:

- their origin (is this a result of tradition, context, technology, relationships with superiors, language?);

WHAT ARE YOUR VALUE SYSTEMS?

IDENTITY	0	1	2	3
reputation				
respect				
success				
honesty				
creativity				
originality				
beauty				
commitment				
character				
generosity				
TOTAL				

RELATIONSHIPS	0	1	2	3
love				
respect				
commitment				
concern for others				
friendship				
education				
obedience				
intelligence				
family life				
morality				
TOTAL				

POWER	0	1	2	3
money				
stubbornness				
cleverness				
success				
social status				
choice				
ambition				
independence				
possession				
revenge				
TOTAL				

OVERALL TOTAL [ ]   OVERALL TOTAL [ ]   OVERALL TOTAL [ ]

In relation to your work, give a mark from 0 – 3:
0: of no importance,   1: of little importance   2: important,   3: very important
to the values listed above according to the degree of significance they hold for you.

55

– their duration and frequency (is this an old habit, well and truly engrained, or a more recent one, or perhaps associated with a particular situation?);
– their effects (positive: security, friendliness, or negative: tensions, rivalry).

At this point, pay particular attention to language use. Studies carried out in the field of neuro-linguistic programming on the key points of language give us some interesting insights.

The diagram below illustrates the different terms to which you should turn your attention.[18]

So, are you mindful of:
– quantitative generalizations: everything, everybody, nobody, never, always, every time, all the time. For example:
  – 'I spoke to everybody' – Was it really everybody? Have you met all your colleagues?
  – 'I've met nobody.' – Really nobody?
– verbs which imply assertion or impossibility without explaining the sense of it: have to, must, want to, able to. For example:
  – 'I had to intervene.' – 'Otherwise what would have happened?'
  – 'He had to correct...' – Otherwise?

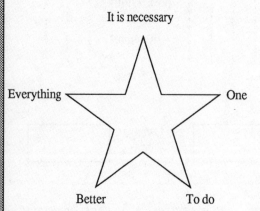

THE FIVE KEY POINTS

It is necessary

Everything — One

Better — To do

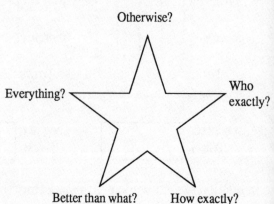

THE FIVE KEY POINTS

Otherwise?

Everything? — Who exactly?

Better than what? — How exactly?

20A

WHAT IS YOUR PROFESSIONAL BEHAVIOUR?

WHAT YOU ARE:

WHAT YOU FEEL:

HOW YOU WOULD LIKE TO APPEAR:

WHAT YOU EVOKE:

WHAT YOU SHOW:

WHAT IS EXPECTED OF YOU:

– words referring to we don't quite know who: one, they, people. For example:

– 'Someone told me...' – Who is this mysterious 'someone'?

– 'They asked me about it...' – Who are 'they'?

– verbs which are not quite specific enough: do, go, see. For example:

– 'I saw Mr X...' – 'To have seen' signifies what exactly; you surely did something else besides see Mr X?

– 'I'm going to prepare this report...' – How exactly?

– omissions of comparison: better, more, less, best... For example:

– 'I got less work done...' Less than what? In relation to what?

This language analysis will help you to develop a more critical outlook by emphasizing your positive habits, which can be adjusted or improved, and your failings.

Thus, you have identified a number of pointers to good professional behaviour or, conversely, some bad habits.

SIX QUESTIONS ABOUT
YOUR PROFESSIONAL BEHAVIOUR

AT WORK

☞ Do you find yourself in agreement:
– with yourself (your expectations, convictions, beliefs)?
always ❑   often ❑   sometimes ❑   never ❑

– with others (what they expect of you)?
always ❑   often ❑   sometimes ❑   never ❑

☞ What kind of person are you? Do you prefer:
– the theoretical?   yes ❑   no ❑   ? ❑
– the technical?   yes ❑   no ❑   ? ❑
– the 'people' aspects?   yes ❑   no ❑   ? ❑

☞ Do you find it difficult to adapt?
always ❑   often ❑   sometimes ❑   never ❑
What are the reasons for these difficulties?

☞ Do you feel you are conservative or, on the contrary, innovative?
conservative ❑   somewhere between the two ❑   innovative ❑

☞ Do you get positive reactions from your colleagues?
most of the time ❑   sometimes ❑   rarely ❑

☞ Do you think you will have to consider changing your professional behaviour?
yes ❑   no ❑   ? ❑
If so, what changes do you envisage making?

YOUR PROFESSIONAL PLAN

Now it is time to take an overview of your study by summarizing and putting together the component parts of your work. You have gradually revealed its positive and negative aspects, and the satisfactions and dissatisfactions on which your feelings of stability are based. During the course of your study you have progressed from asking the question 'How do I function in a professional sense?' to 'Why do I function in this way?'

You have gathered a lot of raw material which you have subsequently clarified, classified and organized. You have carried out a survey of your professional environment by responding to the questions 'Why? Where? How? With whom?' At this stage you probably feel like going back over certain things. If this is the case, go over your notes again, and take time looking over your answers to the various questionnaires in order to benefit from hindsight. Some things can escape you the first time, and it is also possible for responses to vary depending on the time when they are given;

there is always an arbitrary element. Then you will be ready to get your overall professional portrait ready by reaffirming:
– your principal objectives;
– your acquired knowledge;
– productive and non-productive factors;
– your dominant qualities and failings;
– your difficulties;
– your satisfactions and disappointments;
– your relationships and your positive and negative feelings.

You will then be in a position to state what you like and dislike about all this, and what you would like to change about it.

You are in a position to study the results obtained not only in relation to your skills and the means available to you, but also in relation to your usual performance and social climate. You can evaluate the factors which generate harmony or discord physically as well as on the intellectual, pyschological and inter-personal levels. You will become aware of the impact of your work on the rest of your life by determining the way in which it expresses itself in other areas: family, social, cultural and ideological.

WHAT ARE YOUR HABITS?

NATURE	ORIGIN	DURATION/ FREQUENCY	PEOPLE INVOLVED	EFFECT(S)

- Is it something which develops, enhances, or, conversely, does it restrict and stifle?
- Does it favour non-professional activities or is it incompatible with a certain way of life?
- Does it represent an enriching cultural and human factor for you or is it limiting?

You can use a questionnaire for this, to integrate all the different elements which make up your professional situation, and identify the underlying *motives* for your actions. 'By studying the *how* of a behaviour, criterion or strategy we easily gain instant access to the *why,* and we apply the distinctions which make apparent the time framework (past, present and future) and the link between cause and effect.'[19]

The rationale of your situation lies in the relationship between what you have done, what you are in the process of doing and what you are going to do. You will, in this way, evaluate:

- your *obligations*: are they few, acceptable, too many? Do you feel overwhelmed or stressed out by them?
- your *needs*: are they few or too many? Are they important in terms of dependence?
- feelings of *guilt* or regret: do these feelings occupy your thoughts sometimes or are you obsessed by them?
- your *confidence* in your level of competence, your degree of self-confidence: are you sure of yourself and your potential, or do you feel weighed down by your failings?
- your *hopes*: are you optimistic or pessimistic about your professional future?
- possible feelings of *disappointment* or inadequacy: do you feel enriched, comfortable or frustrated, with the impression that you could have done better?
- your *ambitions*: do you present yourself as somebody who is ambitious or career-minded? Are you motivated by your work?
- setbacks or *rejections*: are there things which trouble you or that you have taken badly in your professional life?
- how you *project* yourself: do you have serious ambitions? Do they seem realistic to you or pipe-dreams?

DRAW UP YOUR PROFESSIONAL SELF-PORTRAIT

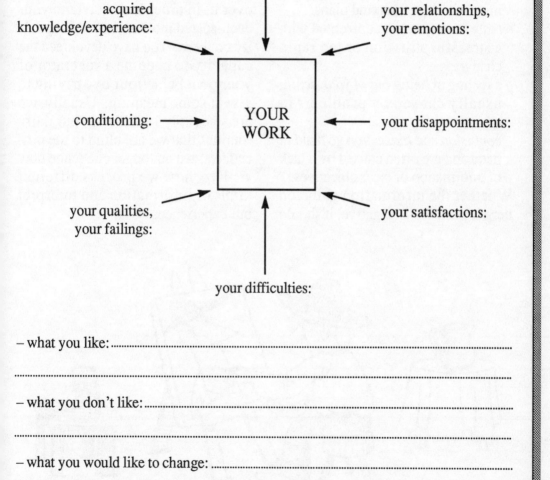

your principal objectives:

acquired
knowledge/experience:

your relationships,
your emotions:

conditioning:

YOUR
WORK

your disappointments:

your qualities,
your failings:

your satisfactions:

your difficulties:

– what you like: ....

....

– what you don't like: ....

....

– what you would like to change: ....

....

Other inner states may be discovered at the same time, such as:

– *despair*, linked to a deep-rooted sense of failure, the certainty that you have mishandled your professional life.
– *boredom*, often caused by routine, lack of novelty or perhaps the impossibility of making plans.
– *fear*, anxiety when confronted with a stressful situation or too rapid change.
– a feeling of being *out of your depth*, usually caused by problems in adjustment.
– *confusion* and *indecision* go hand in hand and are often caused by a lack of information or clear objectives.

Whether the information gathered here is positive or negative, it should be dealt with and used to 'reformulate' your professional practice. The questions will help you to clarify your professional situation, not justify it. Remember that this process is unique to each individual. You are not robbing your practice of its originality, you are casting a critical eye over it, in order to understand your deep-seated motivations and capitalize on them. You have developed the capacity to become a spectator of your own behaviour by striving to give it some meaning. Usually, we are so deeply involved in our daily routines that we are blind to the procedures; we no longer challenge how we live, how we process different kinds of information and interpret our experiences.

WHAT KIND OF RELATIONSHIP DO YOU HAVE WITH YOUR JOB?

	YES	NO	MORE OR LESS
WORK AND YOUR PERSONAL INVOLVEMENT:			
Did you choose your job?			
Do you achieve your aims?			
Do you get the results you hoped for?			
WORK AND RESOURCES:			
Are there enough personnel?			
Is the equipment suitable?			
Are working conditions favourable?			
WORK AND SOCIAL ATMOSPHERE:			
Is there a pleasant atmosphere at work?			
Do you have enough human contact?			
Do you have good professional relationships?			
WORK AND MATERIAL CONSIDERATIONS:			
Is your salary appropriate?			
Are the hours reasonable?			
Are the travel demands acceptable?			
WORK AND YOUR HEALTH:			
Is your work physically or psychologically tiring?			
Does it give rise to health problems?			
Is it possible to recuperate, to recover your strength?			
WORK AND YOUR PRIVATE LIFE:			
Is there a healthy balance between work and family life?			
Does work allow time for a social life?			
Do you have enough free time?			
WORK AND IDEOLOGY:			
Does your job provide cultural enhancement?			
Do you agree with its values?			
Are you fulfilled?			

WHAT ARE THE DETERMINING FACTORS OF YOUR PROFESSIONAL STRATEGY?

restrictions – obligations	– I had to
	– I have to
	– I will have to or I would have to
need	– I needed or I needed to
	– I need or I need to
	– I will need or I will need to
guilt, regret	– I should have
	– I could have
	– I would have needed or I would have needed to
competence, confidence	– I can
hope, optimism	– I will be able to
disappointment, inadequacy	– I was able to
	– I wanted or I would have wanted
ambition, motivation	– I want
refusal	– I don't want
looking ahead, desire	– I would be able to
	– I would like to
	– I would need or I would need to

Section 6
MAKE THE MOST OF YOUR PROFESSIONAL BEHAVIOUR

> *'Some people think that to be yourself is to be static; being yourself seems to them to be synonymous with always being the same. Nothing could be further from the truth. In fact, being yourself secures mobility.'*
>
> Carl ROGERS

The work that you have done in the preceding pages has enabled you to get your bearings by:
– thinking about what you do and the way in which you carry out your various tasks;
– differentiating between what is important and what is superfluous;
– questioning the efficiency of your way of doing things;
– examining your relationships at work.

You shouldn't stay fixed in your current attitudes; instead, take advantage of this self-management procedure to rethink and re-adjust your professional situation. The terms 'high performance' and 'excellence' have entered into management 'lingo' in recent years, but it is not necessary here to go to extremes. Just allow your attention to be drawn to possible improvements in your activities by reviewing your methods and personal organization from a developmental perspective. Work 'is not a curse, it is a necessity of life and implies a desire for social integration and participation.'[20] It requires us to be organized with a view to being more rational, more efficient – this will bring us maximum satisfaction.

In this context, this analysis can be applied to creating a positive attitude. Our study should lead us to manage our professional life better, in other words to:
– maximize our full potential;
– improve the quality of our professional performance;
– free ourselves from unproductive conditioning;
– reprogramme certain aspects of our behaviour;
– prepare ourselves for change.

FORESEEABLE CHANGE AND MOTIVATION

At this point you should list your professional objectives in the short and long term:
– what you must do to reinforce your position;
– what you want to do to attain your ideal.

You will thus be able to think about foreseeable development plans or training. On the one hand, these projects will be linked to obligations and essential needs and, on the other hand, to your ambitions, desires and interests. At this level, where choices have to be determined, you can put your projects into three categories:
– indispensable;
– optional but desirable;
– superfluous.
The expansion of your professional horizon can be illustrated by a spiral, highlighting necessary changes rather than the superfluous. You can visualize your future by imagining perfect performance in a perfect environment. You can measure the gap between this imaginary forecast and reality, and can set priorities to be dealt with in more detail. Having dealt with your main projects, it is wise to clarify your motivation in order to concentrate on what is essential.

WHAT ARE YOUR PROFESSIONAL OBJECTIVES?

TO HOLD DOWN YOUR PROFESSIONAL POSITION, YOU MUST:	TO ACHIEVE YOUR PROFESSIONAL IDEAL, YOU WANT:

– in the short term:

– in the short term:

– in the longer term:

– in the longer term:

Do these needs or desires correspond to:
- *security* (physical, material or moral security; job stability and/or consistency; company reliability and/or reputation);
- a *pleasant atmosphere* (good team spirit, good relationships with superiors, helpful peers);
- a feeling of *well-being* (physical comfort, interesting work, fun);
- *status* (recognition, respect, power);
- *novelty* (intellectually stimulating, personal, social or professional development, varied, non-routine tasks);
- personal *efficiency* (promotion, advancement, higher pay) or company efficiency (better results, product quality, sound finance).[21]

MEANS AND SOLUTIONS

You must move on from the 'why?' to the 'how?' by asking yourself about means and solutions, what efforts you have to make and in what way. Every project has a different degree of difficulty but always involves compromise between your ambitions/interests and reality, the means at your disposal and the restrictions. Conditions for success need to be envisaged in terms of professional environment, of compatibility for:
- yourself;
- your function;
- your team;
- your company.

You have to ask yourself what your expectations are and what others expect of you; in other words, what is the relationship between your objectives and those of your team and the company?
- will these projects make you feel completely fulfilled?
- what degree of freedom is open to you?
- are the restrictions significant?
- what are your future prospects with the company?

HOW DO YOU SEE YOUR FUTURE?

SUPERFLUOUS CHANGES:

....

....

....

DESIRABLE CHANGES:

....

....

....

ESSENTIAL CHANGES:

....

....

....

....

....

....

TODAY

Conflicts may arise to delay the realization of your plans, whether personal (incompatibility of your professional plans with your family life, for example) or with others (peers, superiors). The role played by members of your team is a crucial point here, whether it is a case of the influence exerted on you by one or more individuals acting independently or group pressure. Their contribution may prove to be positive or negative, encouraging or obstructive. Other people can help you in various ways:
- by arousing your natural curiosity;
- by encouraging or stimulating you;
- by helping you through the whole process, so perhaps becoming people to emulate;
- by listening to you, allowing you to put your experiences into words. 'Actually voicing our thoughts and feelings aloud helps us to see them from another perspective';[22]
- by questioning you and forcing you to study certain aspects further;
- by guiding you and relaying information;
- by appraising you.

Unfortunately, our team is not always this helpful and can even be a hindrance:
- by discouraging or denigrating your projects;
- by putting obstacles in your path;
- by withholding the necessary means to your making headway;
- by sidetracking your project from its original objectives;
- by not respecting your ideas or your value system;
- by setting up as rivals or even as enemies.

Mature reflection will allow you to judge the feasibility of your projects and ask yourself:
- what you want to change about your work;
- what you don't want to change;
- what you can change;
- what you can't change.

You will then be in a position to foresee the possible consequences of your actions for yourself, your colleagues and for the company, and so take a decision.

Now is a good time to establish staggered objectives with firm deadlines. Bearing in mind your final and interim objectives, it will then be a case of getting yourself organized:
- planning procedures;
- fixing priorities;
- thinking up related activities (research, courses);
- keeping track of the limitations involved.

We must emphasize the necessity of

WHAT ARE YOUR PRIORITY PROJECTS?

Projected change(s) 'what?'	Reasons 'why?'	Means and solution(s) 'how?'	Level of compatibility for				Realistic conse-quences	Decision(s) date(s) effective 'when?'
			you	your function	your team	your company		
			Score: + favourable 0 unimportant - unfavourable					

evaluating your progress. A regular check is a must in order to assess what has actually been put into operation or abandoned. This will allow you to make any necessary adjustments, assuming, of course, that you have clearly defined from the start what you hope to attain and in what time-span.

TOWARDS DAILY EFFICIENCY

Making the most of your performance demands a particular mental attitude, a willingness to change. We all, no matter what our experience, have untapped resources buried somewhere in us. Therefore, we have to learn to find and exploit this, to fulfil our potential and intensify our way of life. We have to create the necessary favourable conditions for this by concentrating on what is essential once we have clarified our priorities. You have drawn up your professional strategy; now you have to capitalize on it, to become the subject of your self-development. Here are a few guidelines:

– don't allow yourself to be confined by yourself (your past, your habits) or by others;
– don't be over-ambitious by aiming too high;
– let improvements happen gradually;
– learn to tune into your personal energy, your biorhythms;
– introduce changes in your behaviour in order to 'break' with routine (routine gives a false sense of security linked to the feeling of having mastered a particular task);

28

WHAT ARE YOUR RESOLUTIONS?

Note below your principal resolutions to make the most of your performance:

- don't let yourself become immersed in daily matters without sometimes taking an overview;
- make a list of all those 'lost' moments and organize yourself to use them more efficiently (eg have a notebook or something to read handy in your car; you will avoid the stress caused by traffic jams... keep articles or post to read during unavoidable delays);
- observe your surroundings critically;
- sharpen your curiosity by being on the look-out for everything, everywhere: listen, read, look, take note;
- find your 'comfort zone', the mode of behaviour with which you feel most at ease;
- respect other people's experience;
- pay attention to the small details which enhance relationships, products or services;
- apply yourself to setting up new systems;
- don't be discouraged at the first sign of failure or difficulty;
- develop your powers of imagination and creativity without judging yourself too quickly.

This enhancement of your performance can be described as a clarification of your professional projects which adhere to the demands of your job. It is a case of plotting your own individual course, while adhering to your job function, and it means thinking hard about your own projects and the need to adapt. Here you have to maximize your potential and develop your skills, all the while responding, if possible, to your job objectives and your place in your team or organization.

Section 7
DO YOUR SELF-EVALUATION

> *'As individuals, we should not be content simply to become like everybody else.'*
>
> BUSCAGLIA

At this stage in your study, it is a good idea to stop and analyze your reactions to the process of self-evaluation. The difficulties you have faced, the problems you have been confronted with are, in fact, windows revealing your state of mind, the headway you still have to make, the problems you have to wrestle with and the limits to which you have to push yourself.

Evaluation of your performance may entail a number of drawbacks, some linked to the individual and others to the company. In order that this procedure, sometimes the cause of much anxiety – insecurity when faced with an unknown situation, fear of being judged by other people, fear of not understanding, fear of what you might find out – may be introduced gradually into your normal professional behaviour, several conditions are necessary:

- to be motivated;
- to learn to say 'I';
- to be objective;
- to take your time;
- not to feel that you have constantly to justify yourself;
- to be positive.

•
BE MOTIVATED
• •

In order to embark on a self-assessment study, the subject must really want to do it; in other words, to understand the 'why' of the exercise and to appreciate its meaning. We are touching on a twofold problem here: one of mental attitude and of maturity. People are not always prepared for this type of exercise; it may be viewed as judgement if it involves outside intervention, and as 'self-centredness' if it is a self-analysis. The usual types of reaction are as follows:
– 'What's it for?'
– 'I've always managed to do my work without that!'
– 'What will this do?'

Efforts to raise awareness about this new type of job management are therefore crucial. It is also a fact that, within a company, an employee wants to see the results and the changes brought about by evaluation; if not, he quickly becomes demotivated. It is therefore essential to be able to see the 'before' and 'after', to ensure that preparation is the uphill slope (meetings to raise awareness, use of documentation, charts, etc) and follow-up is the downhill slope (following through on steps to fulfil specified objectives).

PERSONAL NOTES

29A

DO AN EVALUATION OF
YOUR SELF-EVALUATION

☞ From the outset of this exercise, are you convinced of the usefulness of self-assessment?

Yes ❑   No ❑   ? ❑

☞ If not, why not? ....

☞ Are you used to self-analysis?

Yes ❑   No ❑

☞ Are you afraid of not being objective?

Yes ❑   No ❑

☞ Have you devoted enough time to completing these exercises?

Yes ❑   No ❑

☞ Would you prefer not to analyze certain things related to your work?

Yes ❑   No ❑

☞ In general are you more:

optimistic? ❑   pessimistic? ❑

In your opinion what are the main reasons for your reluctance about self-evaluation?

LEARN TO SAY 'I'

Analyzing yourself or talking about yourself can seem narcissistic or trite. We often come across this type of worried remark:

- 'I have nothing to say.'
- 'I'm not going to invent things.'
- 'I think it's pretentious.'
- 'I don't think it would be very interesting.'

This kind of modesty must be set aside; nobody can speak for you – you are unique. 'The certainty that there is only one you gives *a priori* value to the most ordinary existence.'[23] Learn to show your originality, the real you. Get rid of any preconceived ideas. Avoid foisting on yourself the conventional image that others expect. Don't try to guess what should or should not be said in order to 'please'. As the evaluation will be carried out in the context of a job review within an organization, the outcome of the exercise is important. It is up to the evaluator to make sure that the person being appraised is at ease, to create an atmosphere which allows free expression; the bottom line is openness, a willingness to listen, tolerance and respect for what the other person has to say. Do not forget, however, that this assessment is supposed to relate to you, to your objectives, to your career, so trying to emulate anyone else would not make sense.

BE OBJECTIVE

Being objective, or not subjective, is not easy. You have to try to describe and analyze your behaviour, not as you perceive it or want it to be.

For this you have to know how to accept uncertainties and imperfections. Avoid all forms of distortion or interpretation of the way things are:

- don't underplay or, conversely, dramatize certain things too much, eg:
  - 'it's not important to…';
  - 'it's a very serious thing to…'
- don't withhold details (they may be of no importance to you but perhaps important to others).
- don't exaggerate, over-elaborate or romanticize by letting yourself be carried away by your own enthusiasm.
- don't make snap or moral judgements, eg:
  - 'it's good!… it's bad!…'
  - 'it's necessary!… I must!…'

☞ If you have finished the work suggested, fill in the form below:

	CHART NO.	TOTALLY	PARTIALLY	NOT AT ALL
SECTION 1	1			
	2			
	3			
	4			
SECTION 2	5A			
	5B			
SECTION 3	6			
	7			
SECTION 4	8			
	9			
	10			
	11			
	12			
	13			
	14			
	15			
	16			
	17			
SECTION 5	18			
	19			
	20A			
	20B			
	21			
	22			
	23			
	24			
SECTION 6	25			
	26			
	27			
	28			
SECTION 7	29A			
	29B			
	29C			
PROGRESS CHART	30			

In order to reach an acceptable level of objectivity, you may find it useful to enlist the help of a neutral third party, someone to play the role of your 'reflection'. Moreover, it is important to choose a working period that gives a true representation of your activity generally. And lastly, make it relevant – don't fix it in time. It represents a stage in your life and as such is valuable at any time.

TAKE YOUR TIME

Taking your time to analyze your performance is not wasting time but gaining time. Lack of time, no time... time is the most frequently used argument for avoiding or delaying a self-assessment study, work that doesn't seem to be top priority in an already full life. Be honest with yourself. Is this excuse of lack of time an alibi or a defence? Any evaluatory process involves questioning things, even making changes and therefore meets with resistance. You may have to 'kiss goodbye' to certain long-held ideas or ways of doing things.

We must also point out that, in the case of company reviews, they are often scheduled to take place at a particular time of the year. This corresponds to a conventional method of organization and allows a 'snapshot' of the company at a precise moment. However, it would be interesting to relax these procedures and introduce the possibility of reviews on demand as the need arises. The review should be considered as an extension of a daily relationship and not as an artificial situation.

☞ For each of the charts which caused you difficulties, try to find out why:

Chart no.

Chart no.

Chart no.

Chart no.

☞ In what areas do you still have to make an attempt at self-evaluation?

☞ How do you envisage completing this work?

DON'T JUSTIFY YOURSELF

This analytical procedure should in no way be perceived as a trial; you are not being asked to justify your performance, only describe it. It is thus desirable for companies to avoid certain adverse effects of appraisals. Salary reviews should be kept separate from these appraisals, otherwise it becomes tempting to alter the evaluation in the light of the foreseen pay rise or manipulate the evaluation criteria. Instead of a procedure aimed at career management based on a climate of mutual trust, the situation declines into a settling of old scores! Morever, the evaluation should be conducted well, with attention paid to badly integrated or understood working systems and techniques. There must be a willingness on the part of the company and a coherent policy. Staff should not feel 'trapped' or 'stressed out' by the new company culture or stretched to their limits, but simply involved in efforts towards motivation and negotiation.

BE POSITIVE

Our social conditioning often leads us to focus on what is wrong – faults, failings, boredom. If you make a mistake at work, you will quickly be told off about it; but if you get things right this is considered normal and passes without comment. So for once, be positive! Reverse the procedure: highlight your strong points, your successes, your good points. It is not a matter of removing all possible problem areas but simply not always highlighting them. Once you have found out what your assets are, you will be better able to confront any difficulties and visualize your progress by adopting a constructive, non-defeatist attitude. There's a solution to every problem!

YOUR PROGRESS CHART

I ✏️

THE PROFESSIONAL'S SELF-ASSESSMENT KIT

CONCLUSION

> *'Each man receives two types of education; one is given to him courtesy of others, the other, much more important, he gives to himself.'*
>
> Edward GIBBONS

'Evaluating people can be considered from two points of view: an 'external' evaluation, which represents the judgement of others on oneself as a function of reference criteria or a scale of values; or an 'internal' evaluation (self-evaluation) which reflects the conscience, the knowledge and the self-esteem of the subject.'[24]

In this book we have chosen to develop the second mode of evaluation, but we must emphasize the fact that one doesn't exclude the other and that the two approaches can be complementary.

In today's world we all participate in change, and research is increasingly important. We are witnessing an end to taylorism, when FW Taylor used to say to his workers, 'You're not paid to think.'

People want their work to make sense, to transcend a situation where they work under compulsion, to one where they work of their own volition. To achieve this they must be responsible for themselves, their words and their actions.

By the type of questions suggested throughout these pages, we have tried to target what one might call professional identity. This involves a motivating process, that is, using the knowledge gained through training and experience and putting it into practice to bring about positive change.

This approach takes on an educational aspect, productive in terms of the individual's new powers of control. It begins at a time of important cultural change: we are witnessing within companies 'an advance from a management system which controls change brought about by successive interruptions, to a system of continuity and development indicating a forward-looking attitude'.[25]

We are working towards a relationship between the employee and his organization within which the individual can adapt to his professional environment. This will result in better management of human resources. It seems crucial to establish a link between new job requirements and the potential and skills of the individuals likely to occupy them. However, if evaluation is a new buzz word, it ought to be accompanied by other terms such as motivation, responsibility and communication.

A company can only demand greater levels of involvement from its staff in a climate of respect, openness and trust. Here we are touching on the problem of changes in mentality and behaviour, and it seems risky to rush things by the use of methods which are unreliable, misinterpreted or badly integrated.

So, softly, softly onwards to a new humanism!

Bibliography

1. Nadeau, J-C (1989) *Éducation permanente*.

2. Ricoeur, P (1990) *Time and narrative*, volume 1, University of Chicago Press.

3. Bourdieu, P (1977) *Outline of a theory of practice*, Cambridge University Press.

4. Eckenschwiller, M (1991) *Mieux se connaître pour trouver un emploi*, Les Éditions d'Organisation.

5. Loquen, L and Merlane, J-C (1990) *L'entretien annuel contaminé par le mérite*, Ressources humaines.

6. Gandrez, H, quoted by R Bazin (1990) *Développement personnel et entraînement mental*, ESF Éditeur.

7. Gusdorf, quoted by J Maisonneuve, *La psychologie sociale*, PUF.

8. Xénakis, F (1976) Le temps usé, Éditions Balland.

9. Hall, E-T (1971) *La dimension cachée*, Éditions du Seuil.

10. Lombart, J-R, and Matouh, A (1989) *Cahiers pédagogiques*.

11. Gittelson, B (1986) *Vos biorythmes*, Éditions Sand.

12. Servan-Schreiber, J-L (1984) *L'art du temps*, Fayard.

13. Nicolas, P, and Mortemard de Boisse, J (1984) *La gestion du temps*, Les Éditions d'Organisation.

14. Roqueplo, P (1974) *Le partage du savoir*, Seuil, Paris.

15. Herzlich, C (1972) *La représentation sociale* in *Introduction à la psychologique sociale*, Larousse, Paris.

16. Cudicio, C (1986) *Comprendre le PNL, La programmation neurolinguistique, outil de communication*, Les Éditions d'Organisation, Paris.

17. Lebel, P (1985) *L'animation des réunions*, Les Éditions d'Organisation.

18. Idem (16), Cudicio.

19. Cudicio, C (1987) *Maîtriser l'art de la PNL*, Les Éditions d'Organisation.

20. Mucchielli, R (1991) *L'étude des postes de travail*, ESF Éditeur.

21. Bazin, R (1990) *Développement personnel et entraînement mental*, ESF Éditeur.

22. Clouzot, O, and Bloch, A (1981) *Apprendre autrement*, Les Éditions d'Organisation.

23. Groult, F *Mémoires de moi*, Édition J'ai lu.

24. Aubret, J (1991) *L'orientation scolaire et professionnelle*, volume 20.

25. Berton, F (1991) *Éducation permanente*.

FURTHER READING FROM KOGAN PAGE

Be An Achiever, Geoffrey Moss, 1991

Great Answers to Tough Interview Questions, Martin John Yate, 1992

Individual Excellence, Ralph Lewis and Phil Lowe, 1992

The Manager's Self-Assessment Kit, Ernst & Young, 1991

Managing Your Time, Lothar J Seiwert, 1989

The Mid Career Action Guide, 2nd edition, Derek Kemp and Fred Kemp, 1992

Moving Up, Stan Crabtree, 1991

The Organised Executive, Stephanie Winston, 1989

Self-Empowerment, Sam R Lloyd and Christine Berthelot, 1992

Test Your Own Aptitude, 2nd edition, J Barrett and G Williams, 1990

Working Abroad: The Daily Telegraph Guide to Living and Working Overseas, 16th edition, Godfrey Golzen, 1993

NOTES

NOTES